DISCOVER AND DO!

WEATHER

GET HANDS-ON WITH GEOGRAPHY

Written by Jane Lacey

W

FRANKLIN WATTS
LONDON • SYDNEY

Franklin Watts
First published in Great Britain in 2021
by The Watts Publishing Group
Copyright © The Watts Publishing Group, 2021

 Produced for Franklin Watts by
White-Thomson Publishing Ltd
www.wtpub.co.uk

HB ISBN: 978 1 4451 7735 9
PB ISBN: 978 1 4451 7751 9

Editor: Katie Dicker
Designer: Clare Nicholas
Series designer: Rocket Design (East Anglia) Ltd

Picture credits:

t=top b=bottom m=middle l=left r=right

Shutterstock: Arthit Premprayot *cover/title page l*,
venimo *cover/title page r*, Harvepino 4b, 20b and 32,
KPP 4t, naKornCreate 5tr and 9tr, Lemberg Vector
studio 6b, Sidhe 7m, ommus 7b and 31b, ananaline 8t,
Maria Yfanti 9bl, Dvirus 9bm, aydngvn 10t and 28, Alena
Nv 10b, Axel Wolf 12b, ActiveLines 12m, Arisa_J 14t,
bulatova 14b, Pogorelova Olga 16m, Artur Balytskyi 16b
and 18b, Flat vectors 19tr, TheCreativeBrigade 19bl,
GO DESIGN 19bl, pikepicture 20t and 29b, Phonlamai
Photo 20m, 29t and 32, GavrBY 21br, sbellott 22t
and 30b, Nadiia Korol 23t, Becky Starsmore 23tr, Still
AB 23mr, dfanego 23br, Cheryl Casey 23bm, Adisa
23bl, Roman Sigaev 23ml, DragonTiger8 24t and 31m,
VectorMine 26t and 31t, alaver 26b, AJP 27t, Singh
Virender 27br; Getty: blueringmedia 5tl and 12t, msan10
5br and 24b, nataka 6t and 30t, shoo_arts 8b, dumayne
16t, kbeis 18t, Bigmouse108 22b; Dreamstime: Berk
Aviation 27b.

All design elements from Shutterstock.
Craft models from a previous series by Q2AMedia.

Every attempt has been made to clear copyright.
Should there be any inadvertent omission, please
apply to the publisher for rectification.

Printed in China

Franklin Watts
An imprint of
Hachette Children's Group
Part of The Watts Publishing Group
Carmelite House
50 Victoria Embankment
London EC4Y 0DZ

An Hachette UK Company
www.hachettechildrens.co.uk

WEATHER

GET HANDS-ON WITH GEOGRAPHY

W

FRANKLIN WATTS

LONDON • SYDNEY

CONTENTS

WHAT IS WEATHER? 6

TEMPERATURE. 8

ATMOSPHERE .10

WIND. 12

WATER 14

STORM! 16

EXTREME WEATHER. 18

WEATHER FORECASTING 20

WEATHER AND LIFESTYLES 22

ADAPTING TO WEATHER. 24

CHANGING CLIMATES 26

GLOSSARY 28

QUIZ AND FURTHER INFORMATION 30

INDEX 32

Words that appear in **bold** can be found in the glossary on pages 28–29.

WHAT IS WEATHER?

Weather is what is happening in the air outside. Weather is how hot or cold the air feels, how much the air is moving and how much water is in the air.

When we go outside, we dress for the weather.

Why is weather important?

Weather affects us in all kinds of ways. Too much rain can bring **floods** and not enough rain can cause **droughts**. Warm, sunny days are perfect for camping, but high winds will blow away the tents! A weather **forecast** tells us what type of weather to expect.

Climate

Each area in the world has a particular type of weather pattern over a period of time. This is called the **climate**. Over millions of years, plants, animals and people **adapt** to survive the climate of their area.

Polar bears and penguins have thick blubber and fur or feathers to protect them from a cold climate.

Climate zones

The world is divided into five **climate zones**. The polar zone is always cold, snowy and icy. The cold zone has short, cool summers and long, cold winters. The temperate zone has cool winters and warm summers. In the dry zone there is hardly any rain. The days are very hot and the nights are cold. The tropical zone is hot and wet all year round.

This map shows the world's five climate zones.

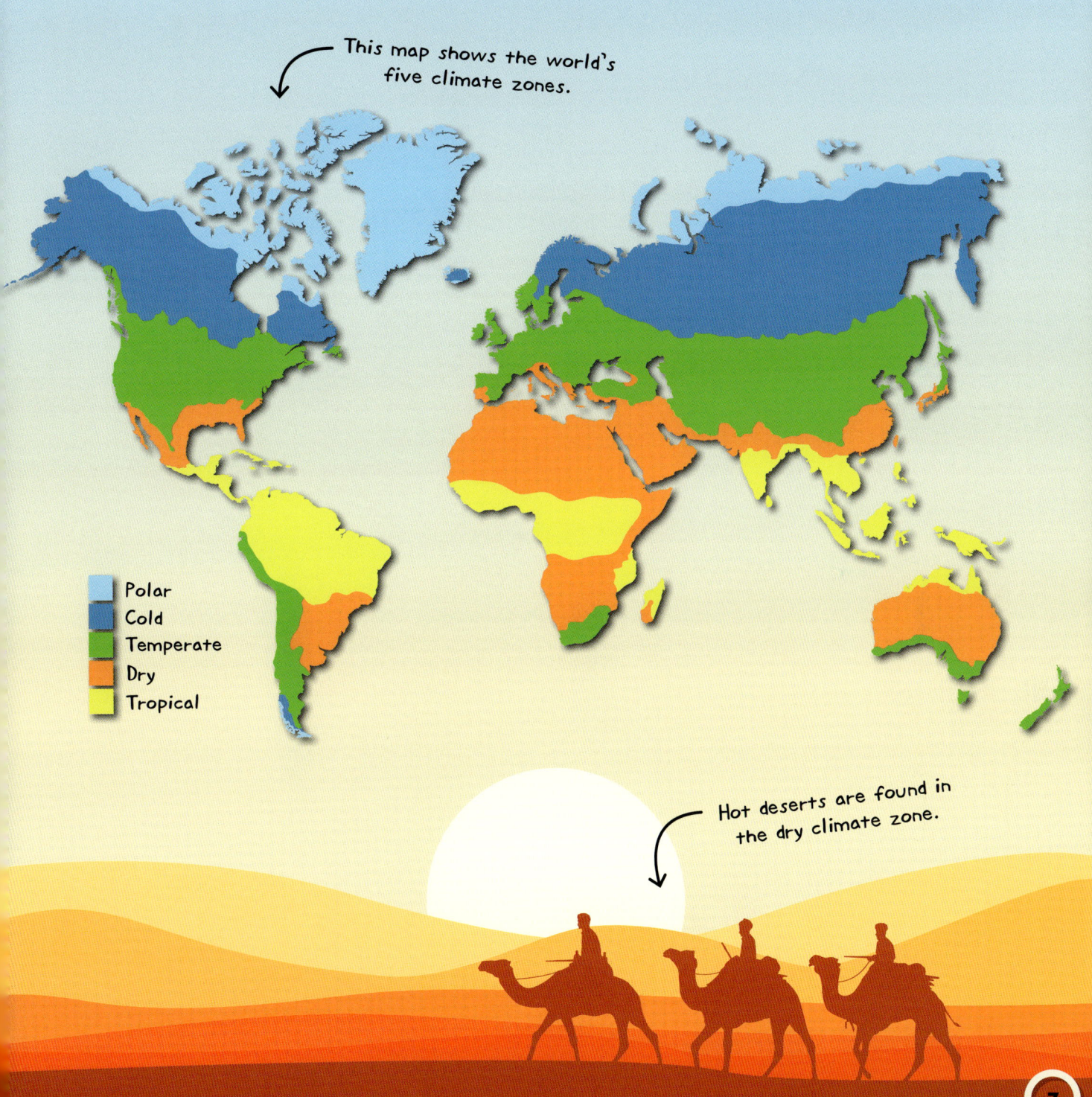

Polar
Cold
Temperate
Dry
Tropical

Hot deserts are found in the dry climate zone.

TEMPERATURE

The temperature is how hot or cold the air is outside. The Sun gives planet Earth its heat. As Earth moves around the Sun, and clouds fill the sky, the temperature changes. We measure temperature with a **thermometer**.

The four seasons bring a cycle of different patterns in weather and nature.

Changes in temperature

During the day, the Sun warms the ground, which heats the air above it. At night, the ground and the air cool down. The air also cools when the Sun goes behind a cloud.

Seasons

Earth takes a year to move around the Sun, spinning as it goes. It is tilted, so the top of Earth points away or towards the Sun at different stages of its journey. This causes the **seasons** to change.

As Earth moves around the Sun, the part tilted towards the Sun has summer, while the part tilted away from the Sun has winter.

Seasons in the Northern and Southern Hemispheres.

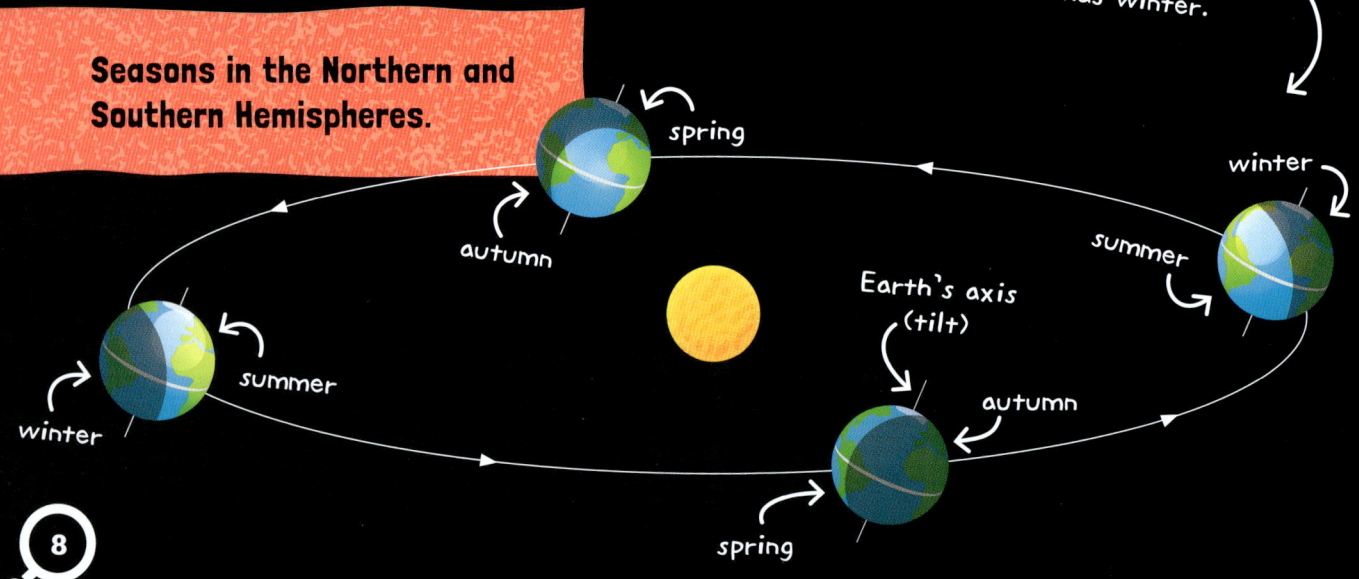

MAKE A TEMPERATURE CHART

You will need:
- **2 garden thermometers (from a garden centre)**
- **notebook**
- **sheet of A5 card**
- **pencil and pens**
- **ruler**

1 Outside, hang one thermometer in a sunny place, the other nearby but in a shady place.

2 On the card, make a chart like the one below. Record the temperature in the sunny and shady places at the same time of day for a week. Mark your temperature and weather recordings on the chart.

	Mon	Tues	Weds	Thurs	Fri
Weather	☀️	🌤️	☁️	🌧️	☁️
Temp 1 Sunny spot	22°C/ 71°F	18°C/ 64°F	15°C/ 59°F	16°C/ 61°F	14°C/ 57°F
Temp 2 Shady spot	18°C/ 64°F	15°C/ 59°F	14°C/ 57°F	15°C/ 59°F	13°C/ 55°F

What do you notice about the temperature changes in the different places?

ATMOSPHERE

Our planet is surrounded by a mixture of gases, dust and **water vapour**, which makes up the **atmosphere**. The atmosphere protects Earth from the Sun's fierce heat and stops warmth escaping into space.

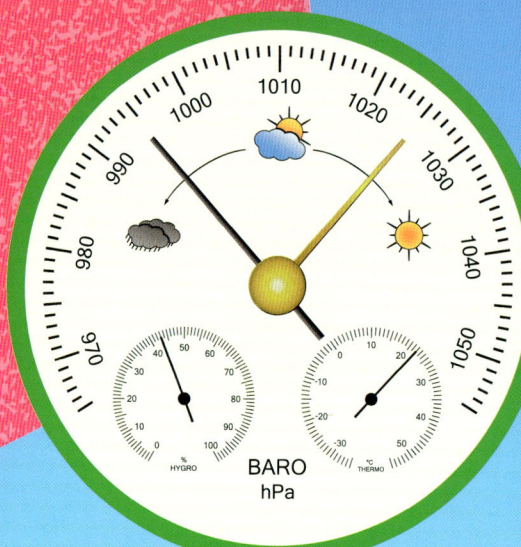

Air pressure is measured with a barometer.

Thick and thin air

The mixture of gases in the atmosphere is called air. Air is thickest and heaviest near the ground. The Sun warms this thicker air and causes it to move as wind. Air spreads out when it rises, so the air becomes thinner higher up.

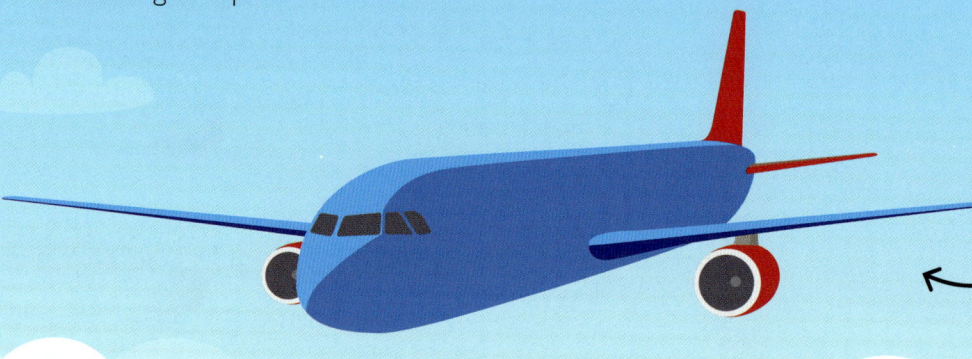

Aeroplanes fly above the clouds where the air is thin and the weather is calmer. This gives a smoother ride.

Air pressure

Even though we can't feel it, air presses down on us all the time. This is called air pressure. When air falls and warms, causing high pressure, settled and sunny weather is on the way. When air rises and cools, with low pressure, it may bring wet and windy weather.

MAKE A SIMPLE BAROMETER

You will need:
- card
- scissors
- felt-tip pens
- sticky tape
- straight drinking straw
- large jar
- balloon
- rubber band

1 Cut a strip of card about 30 cm long and 5 cm wide. Draw a Sun at the top of the card and grey clouds at the bottom.

2 Make a pointer, by cutting a small arrow shape from the card and tape it to one end of the straw.

3 Put the jar on a shelf or windowsill and balance the pointer across the top of the jar. Prop the card up so that the pointer is pointing to the middle of the card. Mark the middle with a line.

4 Cut the neck end off the balloon. Stretch the balloon over the open top of the jar so it is stretched tight and smooth. Secure the balloon with the rubber band. Make sure the jar is airtight.

5 Tape the straw to the middle of the stretched balloon. About 3/4 of the straw should stick out.

6 Put your barometer back on the shelf with the pointer pointing at the card. High air pressure pushes down on the balloon and the pointer rises above the line. Low air pressure pushes less hard on the balloon and the pointer falls below the line.

WIND

Wind is moving air. We can't see wind, but we can feel it as it blows on our skin and hair. We can also see things moving as wind blows against them.

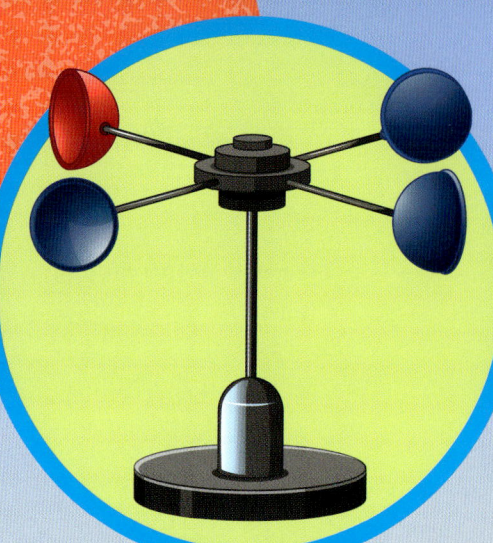

The cups of an anemometer turn to show the speed of the wind.

Moving air

Changes in air pressure keep the air moving. This creates wind. Wind blows from areas of high pressure to areas of low pressure. **Global winds** sweep around the whole Earth. Global westerly winds blow the weather from west to east across North America.

Speed and direction

It can be important to know the speed and direction of the wind. High winds are dangerous for **construction** workers on tall buildings. Strong winds can blow an aeroplane off course or affect an athlete in a race. Wind speed and direction is measured by an **anemometer**.

Big sailing boats use the power of the wind to sail around the world.

MAKE A CUP ANEMOMETER

Ask an adult to help you with this activity

You will need:
- **2 straight drinking straws**
- **sticky tape**
- **4 small paper cups**
- **stapler**
- **drawing pin**
- **sharp pencil with an eraser**

1 Lie the drinking straws so they cross at the centre. Tape them together where they cross.

2 Place a paper cup sideways at both ends of each straw. Make sure they are all pointing in the same direction.

3 Staple the ends of the straws to the tops of the cups near to the rims.

4 Ask an adult to push a drawing pin through the centre of the straws and into the top of the pencil eraser. Hold the pencil and blow into the cups to test that your anemometer spins freely.

Use the anemometer outside to test the speed and strength of the wind. The cups spin quickly in a high wind and slowly in a breeze.

WATER

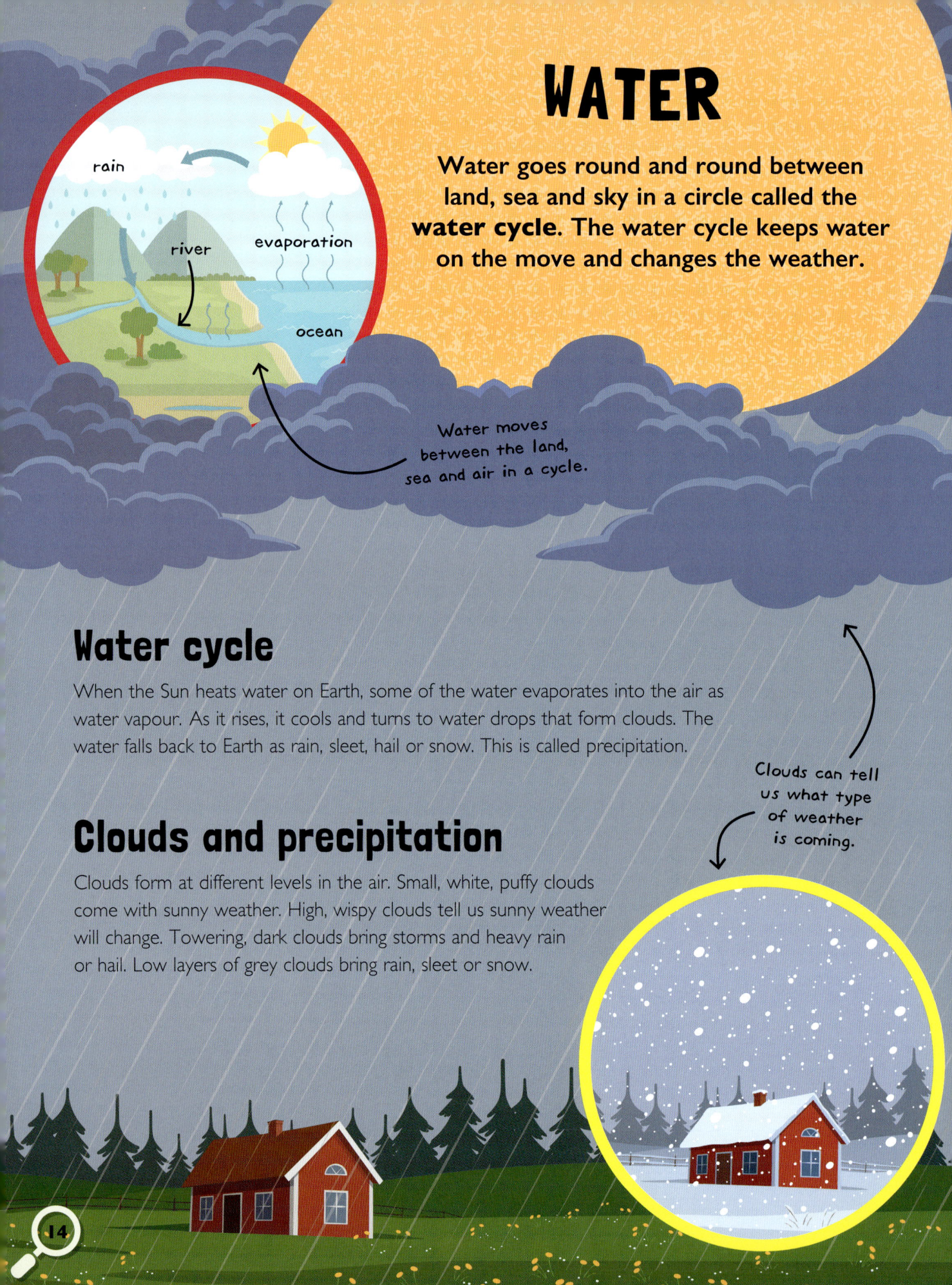

Water goes round and round between land, sea and sky in a circle called the **water cycle**. The water cycle keeps water on the move and changes the weather.

rain

river

evaporation

ocean

Water moves between the land, sea and air in a cycle.

Water cycle

When the Sun heats water on Earth, some of the water evaporates into the air as water vapour. As it rises, it cools and turns to water drops that form clouds. The water falls back to Earth as rain, sleet, hail or snow. This is called precipitation.

Clouds and precipitation

Clouds form at different levels in the air. Small, white, puffy clouds come with sunny weather. High, wispy clouds tell us sunny weather will change. Towering, dark clouds bring storms and heavy rain or hail. Low layers of grey clouds bring rain, sleet or snow.

Clouds can tell us what type of weather is coming.

MAKE A WATER CYCLE CIRCLE

Ask an adult to help you with this activity

You will need:
- **2 large circles of card**
- **pencil**
- **ruler**
- **pens**
- **extra card**
- **scissors**
- **sticky tape**
- **paper fastener**

1 Use the pencil and ruler to divide one circle into six equal segments.

2 Copy the template below to draw the stages of the water cycle in each segment. Label each segment and colour the pictures.

3 Take the second circle of card and ask an adult to help you cut a window the shape of a water drop. It should be big enough to reveal one segment of the first card circle. Stick a small card tab next to the window.

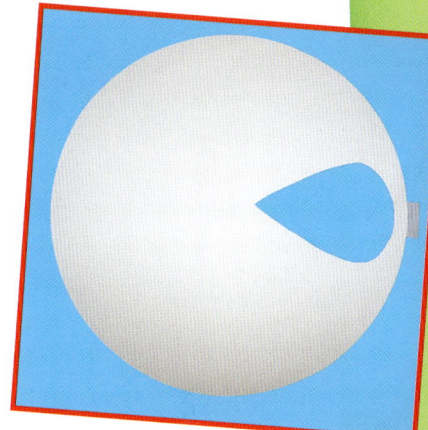

4 Ask an adult to fix the circles together at the centre with the paper fastener. Hold the tab and turn the wheel in a clockwise direction to show water going round in the water cycle.

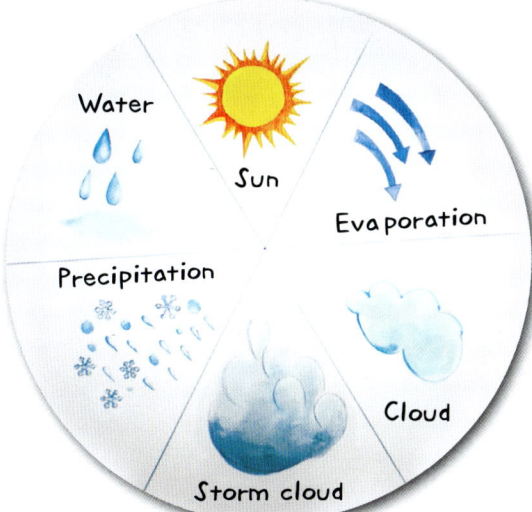

STORM!

A storm is a violent weather event. A storm can have strong winds, heavy rain and hail, blinding snow, thunder and lightning or swirling sands. Storms often cause great damage.

You should stay indoors during a fierce thunderstorm, away from the lightning.

Thunder and lightning

When giant clouds grow like dark towers in the sky on a hot, damp day, a **thunderstorm** could be on its way. Lightning is caused by huge sparks of **electricity** flashing between storm clouds and the ground. It can set fire to trees.

Hurricanes and tornadoes

Hurricanes are huge, swirling masses of wind and rain. They form over the sea and move inland where they can cause terrible damage. A **tornado** is a twisting funnel of air from a storm cloud to the ground. Tornadoes are so strong that they can pick up vehicles in their path.

TORNADO TRICK!

Ask an adult to help you with this activity

Amaze your friends by making a tornado in a bottle.

You will need:
- **2 large plastic bottles**
- **duct tape**
- **sharp pencil**
- **jug of water**

1 Take the lids off the bottles. Cover the spout of one of the bottles with duct tape. Make sure it is watertight.

2 Ask an adult to use the pencil to make a hole (a bit bigger than a hole punch) in the centre of the duct tape over the spout.

3 Fill the other bottle 3/4 full of water and turn the empty bottle upside down on top of it. Tape the two bottles together and check for leaks.

4 Turn the bottles so the bottle with water is on the top. Swirl the bottles gently and watch the water form a water tornado effect in the top bottle, with a tube of air running through the middle of it.

EXTREME WEATHER

When certain types of weather come together at once, they can form extreme weather conditions. Extreme weather can be very dangerous for people, animals and plants.

In drought conditions, it's difficult for plants and animals to survive.

Floods and drought

Rain doesn't fall evenly all over Earth. Some areas have very little rain, while others have rain most days. When there is too much rain, rivers can flood, destroying crops and making water dirty and dangerous to drink. Too little rain causes drought. Crops die and people become hungry and thirsty.

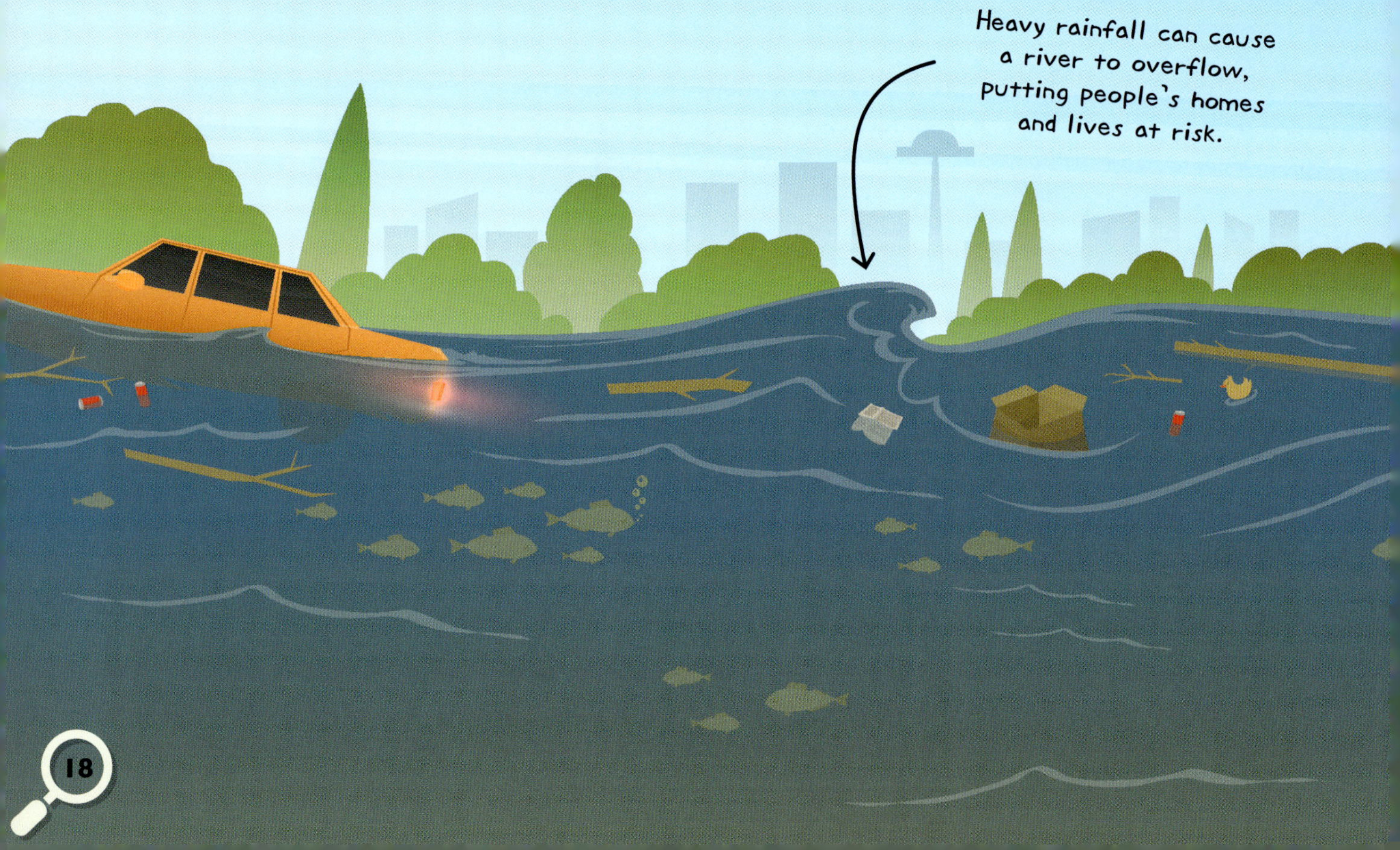

Heavy rainfall can cause a river to overflow, putting people's homes and lives at risk.

Extreme hot and cold

A **heatwave** happens when the land and air heat up and the temperature becomes unusually high. In freezing temperatures, rain can turn to hail, sleet or snow. High winds whip snow into a blizzard.

Blizzard conditions make driving difficult.

MAKE SOME SNOWFLAKES

Every snowflake is different but they all have six points.

You will need:
- **squares of white paper (of different sizes)**
- **pencil**
- **scissors**
- **glue**
- **large sheet of dark blue paper**
- **glitter**

1 Fold the squares in half and then in half again to make smaller squares.

2 Find the corner that is the centre of the square when it is opened out. Turn the folded square so this corner is bottom left.

3 Copy the snowflake shape shown in the template and cut it out along the black lines. Try out some shapes of your own on the other squares.

Template

4 Stick your snowflakes onto the blue card. You can add dabs of glue and sprinkle on glitter for a frosty effect.

WEATHER FORECASTING

Weather forecasting gives us information about what weather we can expect. Knowing what the weather is going to be like helps us to plan a day out.

Weather check

The weather is constantly checked around the world. **Satellites** above Earth collect information about the weather from space. This information is sent to computers to help weather forecasters work out future weather conditions.

Weather forecasts can predict the weather for the week ahead.

A weather satellite takes photographs and measures the temperature on Earth.

Weather science

Weather forecasters study Earth's atmosphere and its effects on weather conditions. They show us what weather to expect in the next few hours or days in a particular area. They have a difficult job because the weather is always changing.

MAKE YOUR OWN WEATHER STATION

Ask an adult to help you with this activity

Make your own weather station. You already have a barometer, anemometer and thermometer from previous activities, now add a rain gauge.

You will need:
- **large plastic bottle**
- **duct tape**
- **ruler**
- **waterproof pen**

1 Ask an adult to cut the top third off the bottle. Turn the top of the bottle upside down. Put it into the bottom of the bottle to make a funnel. Tape around the top with duct tape.

2 Stick a strip of tape up the side of the bottle. Use the ruler and waterproof pen to write on a scale in centimetres from the bottom to the top of the tape.

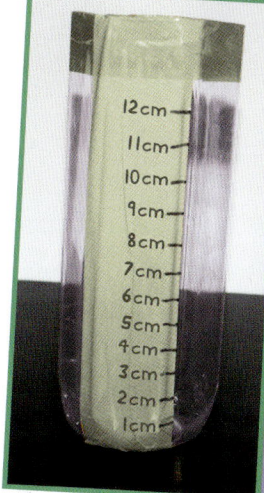

3 Place your rain gauge outside in the open. You could wedge it between stones to stop it blowing away.

4 At the same time each day, record the amount of water collected in the bottle. Then empty it. Check the air pressure, wind speed and temperature in the same area. Record your findings on a chart. Can you use your results to predict the weather for the following day or week?

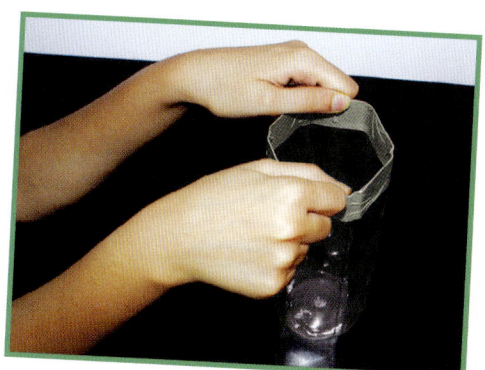

	Mon	Tues	Weds	Thurs	Fri
Amount of rain	1 cm	0 cm	0.5 cm	0 cm	1 cm
Air pressure	low	low	low	medium	low
Wind speed	medium	low	medium	low	medium
Temperature	16°C/61°F	15°C/59°F	16°C/61°F	17°C/63°F	16°C/61°F

WEATHER AND LIFESTYLES

The type of weather in a particular area affects the lifestyle of the people who live there, and the type of plants that grow in the area. People often go on holiday to experience different weather.

Oranges grow well in the warm Mediterranean climate.

The Mediterranean

The weather around the Mediterranean Sea is hot and dry in summer and warm and wet in winter. People spend lots of time outdoors. The weather is just right for farmers to grow fruit, such as grapes, oranges and lemons.

Cold climate

In the cold climate of northern North America and northern Europe and Asia, the summers are short and cool, and the winters are long and cold. In some city centres, shopping malls are underground. This helps people to avoid the harsh winter weather.

Underground shopping centres are useful in cold winter climates.

PLAN A DAY OUT

1 You are going on a class trip. Decide where you want to go – perhaps to the seaside or the mountains. Find your destination on a map.

2 Find a weather forecast in a newspaper, on television, on the radio or the Internet to find out what weather to expect.

3 How will the weather affect your plans?
a) What will you wear?
b) What activities will you do?
c) What equipment will you need?
d) How will you get there?

How will you alter your plans if the weather changes?

www.forecast247.com

Weather Forecast

Home
Travel
Photos
Map

A warm start with a few showers. The afternoon will become brighter and mostly dry with sunny intervals.

ADAPTING TO WEATHER

The design of the houses people live in, the clothes they wear, what they eat and drink, and the jobs they do are all affected by the local weather.

Houses and clothes

Where it is cold all year round, houses have sloping roofs for the snow to slide off. People keep themselves warm by wearing thick clothes. In a hot, dry climate, houses have small windows to keep out the Sun. People prefer to wear loose, light clothes.

Sun umbrellas are used to protect skin from ultraviolet rays in hotter climates.

Some people who settle in or near the mountains work as ski instructors.

Jobs and tourism

Where there is warm sunshine, tourists come to sunbathe and swim. People work in the mornings and evenings and rest in the heat of the day. Where there is plenty of snow in winter, people enjoy sports such as skiing and sledging.

MAKE A PAPER PARASOL

Ask an adult to help you with this activity

You will need:
- coloured pens
- large and small circle of stiff coloured paper or card (20 cm across and 8 cm across)
- sharp pencil
- ruler
- scissors
- bead
- thin stick, 20 cm long
- glue
- sticky tack

3 Stick the first and last folds together to make the shape of your parasol shade.

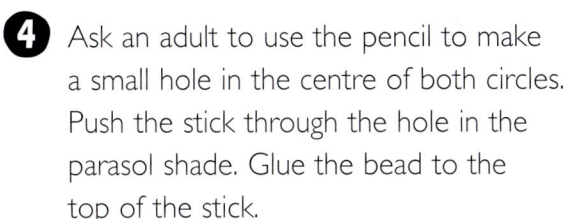

1 Use the coloured pens to decorate the large circle. Draw a line from the side to the centre of the circle and cut along it.

4 Ask an adult to use the pencil to make a small hole in the centre of both circles. Push the stick through the hole in the parasol shade. Glue the bead to the top of the stick.

5 Press sticky tack around the stick beneath the parasol shade to hold it in place. Push the small circle up to the top of the stick to open the parasol. Pull it down to close it again.

2 Fold a section of the circle so it is pointed at the centre and about 1.5 cm wide at the edge. Make repeated folds back and forth all the way round the circle as if you were making a fan.

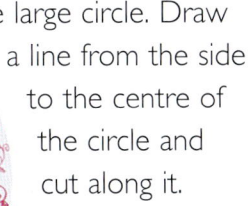

CHANGING CLIMATES

The climate on our planet has been changing very gradually over millions of years. Now it is changing more quickly because of things people are doing all over the world.

Global warming

Fumes from **exhaust pipes**, factory chimneys and power stations send gases into the air. They are called **greenhouse gases** because they trap the heat of the Sun, like the glass in a greenhouse. These gases contribute towards rising temperatures on Earth. We call this **global warming**.

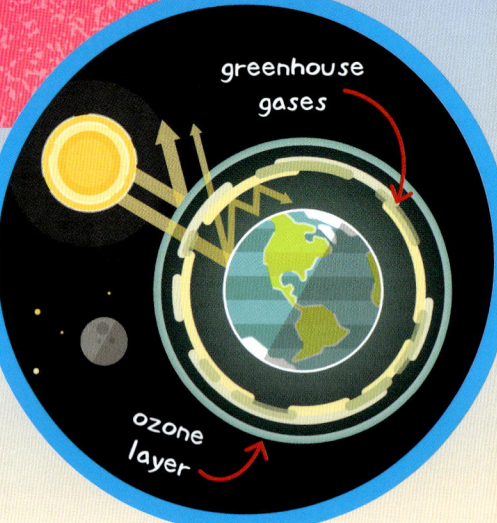

greenhouse gases

ozone layer

Greenhouse gases cause some of the Sun's rays to reflect back to Earth.

Global warming is causing polar ice to melt and sea levels to rise. This could flood low-lying coastal cities such as Venice.

Extreme weather

If global warming continues, we should expect more extreme weather events in the future. There will probably be less cold and frost in some places and more heatwaves and drought in others. Heavier rain will bring more floods and there may be more storms.

India has seen increased flooding in recent years. The state of Kerala was badly affected in 2018.

ACTIVITY

WRITE A NEWSPAPER REPORT

Research a recent extreme weather event using books or the Internet and write a short newspaper article about a similar imaginary event.

a) Describe the weather as it happened.
b) Quote an eye-witness account.
c) Describe what the place looked like after the event was over.
d) What damage was done?
e) What kind of help did the local people need?

Glossary

adapt

Plants, animals and people that adapt have changed over millions of years to survive in their environment.

anemometer

An anemometer is an instrument that measures the speed and direction of the wind.

atmosphere

The atmosphere is the mixture of gases, dust and water vapour that surrounds Earth.

climate

Climate is the type of weather a place has over a long time.

climate zone

A climate zone is a large area that has a particular type of climate.

construction

Construction is the making or building of something.

drought

A drought is a long period of very dry weather when there is not enough rain for crops to grow.

electricity

Electricity is a type of energy. Lightning is a form of electricity.

exhaust pipe

An exhaust pipe is a pipe fitted to a vehicle through which fumes from burning fuel escape.

floods

Floods are caused when rivers become too full and overflow.

forecast

A forecast is a prediction of what might happen in the future, such as a change in the weather.

global warming

Global warming is the gradual increase of the world's temperature. It is partly caused by greenhouse gases in the air.

global winds

Global winds are winds that blow in one direction for long distances around Earth.

greenhouse gas

A greenhouse gas is a type of gas that traps heat from the Sun. Carbon dioxide is one example.

heatwave

A heatwave is a long period of unusually hot weather.

hurricane

A hurricane is a very powerful tropical storm with high winds and heavy rain.

satellite

A satellite is a spacecraft that goes around and around Earth. Weather satellites send information about the weather from space back to Earth.

season

A season is a period of a particular type of weather. The year is divided into four seasons – spring, summer, autumn and winter.

thermometer

A thermometer is an instrument that measures the temperature of air or water, for example.

thunderstorm

A thunderstorm is a storm with thunder and lightning, and often very heavy rain.

tornado

A tornado is a type of windstorm in the form of a funnel of air that spins over land.

water cycle

The water cycle is the movement of water round and round between air, sea and land. Rain falls to the ground and runs into rivers and the sea. Water evaporates into clouds and falls again as rain, sleet or snow.

water vapour

Water vapour is formed when liquid water turns into a gas.

Quiz

1 Which of the following is NOT a climate zone?

a) cold

b) tropical

c) temperate

d) toasty

2 How long does Earth take to move around the Sun?

a) a year

b) a month

c) a week

d) a day

3 When air is near the ground it is:

a) thin and light

b) thick and heavy

c) thin and heavy

d) thick and light

4 Wind blows:

a) from areas of low pressure to areas of high pressure

b) from areas of high pressure to areas of low pressure

c) from areas of no pressure

d) from any areas

5 Heavy rain clouds are usually:

a) small and white

b) high and wispy

c) tall and dark

d) white and puffy

6 Hurricanes form:

a) over the sea

b) over the land

c) up high

d) down low

7 Which of the following are types of precipitation?

a) rain

b) hail

c) sleet

d) snow

8 The weather around the Mediterranean Sea is:

a) hot and wet in summer

b) hot and dry in summer

c) cold and wet in winter

d) cold and dry in winter

9 Which of the following are often found in a hot climate?

a) houses with small windows

b) parasols to provide shade

c) people wearing loose, light clothing

d) a rest from work in the middle of the day

10 Global warming can cause which of the following?

a) rising sea levels

b) heatwaves and drought

c) flooding and storms

d) extreme weather

ANSWERS 1d, 2a, 3b, 4b, 5c, 6a, 7 all of these!, 8b, 9 all of these!, 10 all of these!

FURTHER INFORMATION

BOOKS

Curious Nature: Weather and Seasons by Nancy Dickmann, Franklin Watts

Outdoor Science: Weather by Sonya Newland, Wayland

Natural Disaster Zone: Wild Fires and Freak Weather by Ben Hubbard, Franklin Watts

Wild Weather: Find out how weather and climate affect our world by Liz Gogerly, Franklin Watts

WEBSITES

Learn more about weather and climate www.bbc.co.uk/bitesize/topics/z849q6f/articles/z7dkhbk

Learn how to predict the weather yourself kids.nationalgeographic.com/explore/nature/predict-the-weather

30 freaky facts about the weather! www.natgeokids.com/uk/discover/geography/physical-geography/30-freaky-facts-about-weather

Find out more about weather and test yourself www.dkfindout.com/uk/earth/weather

Index

air 6, 8, 10, 12, 14, 16, 19, 26
air pressure 10, 11, 12, 21
anemometer 12, 13, 21
atmosphere 10

barometer 10, 11, 21
blizzard 19

climate 6, 7, 22, 24, 26, 27
climate change 26, 27
climate zones 7
clothes 24
clouds 8, 10, 14, 16

drought 6, 18, 27

farming 22
floods 6, 18, 27
food 22

global warming 26, 27
greenhouse gases 26

hail 14, 16, 19
heatwave 19, 27
houses 24
hurricane 16, 27

ice 7, 26

jobs 24

lightning 16

rain 6, 7, 14, 16, 18, 19, 21, 27
rain gauge 21
rivers 14, 18

seasons 8
snow 7, 14, 16, 19, 24
sports 24
storm 14, 16, 27
Sun 6, 8, 9, 10, 14, 24, 26

temperature 6, 7, 8, 9, 16, 19, 20, 21, 22, 24, 26, 27
thermometer 8, 9, 21
tornado 16, 17

water 6, 10, 14, 15, 18
water cycle 14, 15
water vapour 10, 14
weather forecast 6, 20, 21, 23
wind 6, 10, 12, 13, 16, 19, 21